Ida and June Hunt for Treasure!

by Katy Wischow • Illustrated by Yoss Sanchez

Lucy Calkins and Michael Rae-Grant, Series Editors

LETTER-SOUND CORRESPONDENCES

all consonants, all short vowels, ll, ss, zz, ck, ch, sh, th, wh, ng, CV words

n(k), tch, a(l, ll), a_e, i_e, o_e, u_e, -es, -ing, -ed, i(nd), -y = /ē/, ea, ee, ai, ay, oa, ow = /ō/, igh, oo, ew, -le, ar, **or**

HIGH-FREQUENCY WORDS

do, his, is, of, says, the, to, was, you

her, your, into, they, are, what, put, from, have, come, some, here, there, don't, know, one

Ida and Jake Hunt for Treasure!
Author: Katy Wischow
Series Editors: Lucy Calkins and Michael Rae-Grant

Heinemann
145 Maplewood Avenue, Suite 300
Portsmouth, NH 03801
www.heinemann.com

Copyright © 2023 Heinemann and The Reading and Writing Project Network, LLC

All rights reserved, including but not limited to the right to reproduce this book, or portions thereof, in any form or by any means whatsoever, without written permission from the publisher. For information on permission for reproductions or subsidiary rights licensing, please contact Heinemann at permissions@heinemann.com. Heinemann's authors have devoted their entire careers to developing the unique content in their works, and their written expression is protected by copyright law. We respectfully ask that you do not adapt, reuse, or copy anything on third-party (whether for-profit or not-for-profit) lesson-sharing websites.
—Heinemann Publishers

"Dedicated to Teachers" is a trademark of Greenwood Publishing Group, LLC.

Cataloging-in-Publication data is on file with the Library of Congress.

ISBN-13: 978-0-325-13900-5

Design and Production: Dinardo Design LLC, Carole Berg, and Rebecca Anderson

Editors: Anna Cockerille and Jennifer McKenna

Illustrations: Yoss Sanchez

Photograph: p. 32 © Jaroslav Moravcik/Shutterstock

Manufacturing: Gerard Clancy

Printed in the United States of America on acid-free paper
3 4 5 6 7 8 9 10 MP 28 27 26 25 24 23
January 2023 printing / PO# 4500866759

Contents

1 The Stormy Day 1

2 On the Hunt 11

3 The Treasure 23

The Stormy Day

Rain, rain, rain.

What a stormy, gray day.

"I don't know what to do!" Ida moans.

"Will you play with me?"

"Sorry," says Mama. "I have to work. Why don't you do a puzzle?"

"*Ug!*" says Ida. "You *know* I don't like puzzles."

"Why don't you read a book?" says Mom.

"I read *all* my books!" says Ida.

Ida flops on the rug
and tries to think.
What is there to do
on such a stormy day?
She thinks of storms
and stormy seas and boats
and gold and—

"I know!" she says.

"Can I go get Jake?

We can have a TREASURE HUNT!"

Ida runs across the hall and knocks on Jake's door. "Jake! Jake! Come on! We're going to hunt for treasure!"

"Cool! Can we dress up?" says Jake.

Ida grins. "YES!"

Ida zips past Mom and Mama.

"We're going on a treasure hunt!" she calls.

"Okay!" say the moms.

"But don't make a mess!"

"Let's see..." says Jake.

"If we're going to hunt for treasure, we need a scarf and a hat and a sword..."

Ida nods. "And we need to make a fort too!"

2
On the Hunt

Ida and Jake are on the hunt for treasure!

They dash into the kitchen.

"Let's start here!" Ida says.

"Look!" yells Jake. "Treasure!"

It's a...

...shiny, new pack of gum! *Yum!*

Jake hands the gum to Ida and says, "Let's put it in the fort!"

They run into Ida's room.

Ida taps a big cardboard box.

"This can be the fort!"

They scramble inside

and hide the gum in the back.

"We got one treasure," says Jake.

"But we need MORE!"

They find a ring...

and some corks...

and a rainbow pin.

And then they see a GREAT treasure—
a tall glass on a high shelf.
It shines and gleams.

"We *need* that glass for the fort!"
says Ida.

"But Ida...that's a *real* treasure!" says Jake.

"Yes," says Ida.

"And we *really* need to get it!"

Jake looks up at the high shelf.

"Yeah, but we're too short to reach it."

"Not me," says Ida.

She steps onto a chair.

She s t r e t c h e s her arm up.

The tip of her hand brushes the glass.

It wobbles…it tips…

"Wait!" yells Jake.

3
The Treasure

"*Whoops!*" gasps Ida.

Jake bites his lip.

"We broke a *real* treasure! Your moms will be *so* mad!"

Mom and Mama run in.

"Oh, Ida! What happened?" says Mom.

They stare at all the bits of glass.

Ida hangs her head.

"We're sorry…" she says.

"We didn't mean to.

I know you told us not to

make a mess, but we did."

Ida gets the broom.

Jake gets the dustpan.

Mom and Mama sweep and sweep until the sharp bits are all gone.

"No more treasure hunt," says Mom.

"And no more fort. Play something safe!"

"Mom *loved* that glass," says Ida.

"It was from her uncle. I feel so bad."

"Me too," says Jake.

They both sigh.

"What can we do
to make it okay?" asks Ida.
They sit on the end of the bed
and think for a long time.

Then Ida jumps up
and runs into the fort.
"I know!" she says.
"We can make a new glass
with all the treasure!"

Ida and Jake hand the gift to her moms. "We are sorry!"

"Oh, look at *this!*" says Mom. "What a treasure!"

Learn about...
Buried Treasure

Is there really such a thing as buried treasure? Yes and no.

King Tut's tomb was discovered in 1922.

There are *some* treasures buried in the ground. Usually these are part of tombs or graves—places where dead people were laid to rest long ago. A famous buried treasure is the tomb of King Tutankhamun. He was the *pharaoh,* or king, of Egypt about 3,000 years ago.

When King Tut died, he was buried along with loads of treasure. The ancient Egyptians believed that if you were buried with your favorite stuff, you could take it with you to heaven.

So yes, there *are* some buried treasures. But, no, there *aren't* really treasure maps that will lead you to buried treasure. You may have heard that pirates liked to make treasure maps, but in real life most pirates didn't bury their treasure—they *used* it to buy stuff like fancy meals and fancy clothes.

Talk about...

Ask your reader some questions like...

- What happened in this book?
- Turn to page 20. If you were Jake, what might you say to Ida to convince her to leave the glass alone?
- Turn to page 25. How is Ida feeling on this page? How do you know?
- What do you like to do on a stormy, gray day?